contents

KU-131-929

shopping for food

Open all hours

Buying food has never been easier. Our shops are bigger and contain a wider variety of goods than ever before. We also have more options when it comes to paying for food. But more importantly, many of us can buy food at almost any time of the day or night. If you fancy a tub of ice cream at 4am just call at your local 24-hour supermarket and take your pick.

Over the last ten years there have been tremendous changes in the way food shops have been owned and run. Fifty years ago lots of small businesses would provide customers with specialist goods in the form of greengrocers, fishmongers, bakers and so on. Today, a large proportion of the food retail market is owned by just a few major companies, and these provide us with an enormous range of goods, all under one roof. Shopping for food has progressed from corner shop to out-of-town supermarket or superstore.

The introduction of supermarkets owned by large companies has often meant that food prices have come down while the quality of food on offer has improved. The sheer size of many supermarkets enables them to run very efficient businesses with well-trained staff and highly technical equipment. They are also able to negotiate good prices for food products because they order in such large quantities. Food is distributed quickly and easily, giving consumers the choice of a wide range of fresh goods from all over the world. Powerful marketing techniques such as customer loyalty cards have also helped supermarkets win customers away from smaller food shops. Customer loyalty cards are used to gain points that can be exchanged for reductions off future payments or for the purchase of other goods or services.

Out-of-town

The main advantage of an out-of-town supermarket or superstore is its convenience. They have their own car parks, which are usually free, with spaces allocated to parents of young children and people with disabilities. For those without transport, a bus service may be offered. Other services available at superstores often include cash machines, dry cleaners, coffee shops, chemists, post offices and even a hairdresser. Staff are usually on hand if a customer requires help with their packing and systems such as 'self-scanning' enable consumers to calculate their bill as they shop. All these innovations have come about because people want a more convenient way to carry out the mundane task of shopping for food.

Paying for food

How we pay for our shopping has also changed significantly in just the last decade. The food bill used to be paid for in cash or perhaps by writing a cheque. Today, cheques can be printed automatically and payment can also be made by debit card, credit card or store card. In each case, all we have to do is check the details and sign our name. Most stores also offer a cashback service.

Food shopping is becoming so convenient we don't even have to leave home to do it! Many supermarkets offer services through which credit cards can be used to

buy groceries over the phone or the Internet. By trawling through the products available on-screen, an order can be placed, paid for and delivered to your door. Your regular shopping list can even be stored ready for future shopping. Although a charge is often levied for these services, many people feel it is worth it for the amount of time they can save.

Consumer spending

There are many reasons why changes have occurred in our retail world and one of these is the overall rise in our standard of living. Generally speaking, people have more **disposable income** and are spending more money on 'luxury items' such as holidays abroad and leisure activities. However, this increase in consumer spending doesn't usually mean people spend more on food eaten in the home. But the type of food demanded by consumers today is certainly changing. People want a wide variety of convenient and high-quality food products.

Out-of-town superstores offer consumers the convenience of having a wide range of goods all under one roof.

Advances in technology have also had a significant impact on the foods we buy and the way in which we shop. Not only are many foods processed so that they can have a long shelf-life but consumers can store foods in a fridge or freezer at home. There is a wide range of frozen foods available, many of which can be cooked from frozen, adding to their convenience. The rise in the number of households with microwaves has led to more microwavable products being consumed than ever before.

Recent technological developments in food packaging, such as **modified atmosphere packaging (MAP)**, has also enabled products to be preserved for longer. Containers can often be used both for cooking and serving food products such as readymeals.

Consumer power

The type of foods available today reflects the foods demanded by a majority of consumers. Demands tend to echo people's lifestyles. Generally, people are busier and want to spend more time on leisure activities than on household chores such as shopping and cooking. Consumers now demand more convenience-type foods and the food industry has responded accordingly. This has involved input from product development, materials and packaging, production engineering, marketing and manufacturing.

The criteria people tend to judge food by when shopping today veers towards quality, convenience and choice. In the past, people often quoted price as an important factor in decision making about food. However, nowadays, if time is short consumers may be prepared to spend a little more money in order to have a product that is convenient. For example, a consumer may be aware that the cost of fruit and vegetables is lower at the town's market. But it may be less convenient and more time consuming to take a separate trip into town (where parking may be difficult or expensive) to buy groceries when the entire weekly shop can be purchased at a superstore.

Of course, although there are trends towards shopping in large stores and buying food in bulk, this does not mean all consumers follow them. People have different needs and wants. For example, there is a current trend towards choosing organic foods and those that have not been **genetically modified**.

Food on the move

As well as having a better standard of living, today's society also enjoys more leisure time. This time is generally due to the advances in technology which help to make household tasks quicker and easier. More of us own automatic washing machines, vacuum cleaners, dish washers, tumble driers, microwave ovens and freezers. Cars make it easier for us to attend leisure time activities such as sports, hobbies and evening classes, or take weekend breaks.

There is also a tendency for people to have busy, hurried lifestyles and eating while on the move, or 'grazing' is the current eating trend. Just thirty years ago, the majority of families would sit round a table and start the day with breakfast. Lunch would probably be eaten at work or school but the day would end together with an evening meal. Today, it is far more likely

◄ *An increasing number of consumers are today choosing to buy organic foods.*

that breakfast is eaten while running for the bus and tea is consumed at different times during the evening, possibly in front of the television or computer. Food products suitable for this lifestyle of grazing include many hand-held products such as breakfast bars, salads supplied with a spoon, ready-made sandwiches and filled tortilla snacks.

Seasonal food

To meet the many demands of today's consumer, the food industry offers a huge range of products which provides customers with an incredible choice. In addition, improved transportation and distribution methods mean foods from all over the world can be purchased from our local supermarket. Without efficient **importation systems** we would not be able to try fruits such as apricots from Turkey, grapefruits from Israel or mangoes from South Africa.

In addition, we are able to eat certain foods all year round. For example, redcurrants are grown in the UK only during the summer months but, by

Organic foods are produced using farming methods that avoid the use of all artificial pesticides and fertilizers, and animals are not routinely given drugs or antibiotics.

importing them from other countries, UK supermarkets are able to offer them at any time of the year (albeit for a higher price than UK redcurrants sold in July). Some consumers feel that by making foods available all the time we lose the value of 'seasonality' (eating foods according to the season in which they are grown).

Fairtrade foods

Fairtrade food schemes have come about following the exploitation of some workers in developing countries who receive extremely poor wages in return for goods sold for a sizeable profit by the manufacturers. The Fairtrade mark is a consumer label that guarantees a better deal for producers in developing countries. An example is the Divine Fairtrade chocolate bar.

types of consumer

Consumer groups

Different types of consumer have emerged over the last decade or so. These pages look at those consumers and the demands they make on today's food industry.

Women

At one time women carried out the majority of food shopping and cooking. Now men are just as likely to shop and cook. This is mainly due to the increased number of women who are working and remaining in work after having children. Women also tend to have fewer children and start their families at a later age. For example, an average sized household in the UK has almost halved from 4.6 people, a fairly constant figure until the early 20th century, to 2.4 people by 1998–99. Since 1992 women aged from 30 to 34 are more likely to give birth than women aged 20 to 24. Household chores have become more of a shared occupation for men and women, so food manufacturers can no longer specifically target women when promoting meals for the family.

Single households

There has also been a significant increase in the number of people living on their own over the last ten years. Today, 29 per cent of households are made up of one person living on their own, as compared with 14 per cent in 1961. Naturally, this has created a whole new **consumer target group** for food manufacturers. Readymeals-for-one are aimed at busy working people who haven't the time (or perhaps the inclination) to prepare a meal when they get in from work.

▼ *Food manufacturers constantly monitor the type of food bought by different consumers. This allows them to meet the needs of the various consumer groups.*

Older people

One reason why the number of single households has increased is because people are living longer. Today, the average man lives to 75 years while the average women lives to be 78. However, in 1911 men could expect to live to about 49 years while women lived until they were 52. Our society is now said to have an 'ageing population' which means we have a greater number of older people in comparison with younger generations. This older group of consumers has different needs and wants from younger people so the food industry has also had to respond accordingly. More single portion meals are now available, particularly of traditional foods such as steamed pudding and shepherd's pie.

Young people

At the other end of the scale, there is a trend for young people to move out of the family home and into a place of their own at an earlier age. In the past, people tended to wait until marriage before leaving home but now young people often want early independence and choose to wait until they are older before getting married, if they decide to marry at all.

Within this consumer target group there has been a decline in their consumption of red meat, especially amongst females. Vegetarianism itself is on the increase and the vegetarian food market in Britain alone was estimated to be worth £1.1 billion in 1997. This may be partly explained by the growing multicultural society and many religions that involve a vegetarian diet. For example, most Rastafarians and Hindus do not eat meat, while Sikhs will not eat beef and Muslims avoid pork.

Children

Although children have not always been seen in terms of a 'consumer group', they are certainly viewed that way today. In the UK, in 2000, KP spent £7 million on the launch of its new brand character for Hula Hoops®, Hoopy McHula (Trademark of United Biscuits UK Ltd). There is growing concern about the way children are the target in advertisements for foods that are high in sugar, salt and fat. Many people now believe advertising such foods during children's television time should be banned.

As young children are not able to judge the nutritional value of foods, they tend to choose food by its appearance and taste. Very often children prefer sweets and snacks which do not necessarily provide them with the necessary nutrients for their growing bodies. When faced with sweets near the checkout counter or advertisements for the latest salty snack, children are bound to put pressure on their parents to buy them.

In June 2000, the Department of Health and the Food Standards Agency published the results of its National Diet and Nutrition Survey of Young People aged four to eighteen years. It showed that children are eating far too few vegetables and fruits and far too much salt. Most children are consuming more **saturated fat** than they should be and too much sugar, mainly in the form of fizzy drinks, chocolate and sweets.

meatless meals

Being vegetarian

Following a vegetarian diet has become increasingly popular but the food eaten by vegetarians can vary enormously. For example, some demi-vegetarians will eat fish and/or white meat while others avoid all animal products including eggs and cheese. For some it is just about cutting out certain foods and for others it is a way of life. In order to clarify the differences within this particular consumer group, categories of vegetarian are used, as outlined in the chart below.

Why vegetarianism?

There is an estimated 3 million vegetarians in Britain alone. Many people believe a diet free from animal products is healthier and give this as their reason for becoming vegetarian. Foods such as meat, butter and cheese contain **saturated fats** which are thought to contribute to the risk of **coronary heart disease**. However, foods that may be found in the diet of a vegetarian are usually low in fat and high in dietary fibre called **non-starch polysaccharide (NSP)**. These include vegetables, wholegrain rice, pulses and **textured vegetable protein (TVP)**.

Concern over food safety has also contributed to a reduction in the consumption of some animal products. Scares such as bovine spongiform encephalopathy (BSE), *Salmonella* and *E.coli 0157* have convinced many people that it is safer to avoid certain foods.

Family tradition or religious belief may also be reasons for becoming vegetarian. Then there are those who do not like the taste, aroma, texture and/or appearance of meat and so choose a meat-free diet. Economy is also given as a reason for vegetarianism. Many vegetarians believe the rearing of animals is an expensive way to feed the population and that land could be put to better use if plants were grown instead of grazing animals. Some people choose a

Classifying vegetarians

Non-meat eaters	Follow a less restricted diet than other vegetarians. Some exclude all types of meat while others cut out red meat only.
Lacto-ovo vegetarian	Do not eat meat, fish or poultry and avoid any ingredients derived from these sources (such as gelatine). They will eat eggs and dairy products.
Lacto vegetarian	Do not eat meat, fish, poultry or eggs and avoid any ingredients derived from these sources. They will eat dairy products.
Vegan	Very strict vegetarians who will not eat any animal product or food derived from animal sources. They also exclude foods and products that involve the use of or the harming of animals (such as leather clothes and shoes).

▲ *Vegetarians can obtain sufficient protein from a diet that includes nuts, pulses, soya milk and tofu.*

vegetarian diet because they do not believe in killing animals for human consumption. They also feel that animals are exploited by intensive farming methods.

Essential nutrition

To stay healthy we all need to ensure that we are following a nutritionally balanced diet. It is important for vegetarians to include certain nutrients that may be lacking if their diet excludes meat and other animal foods. These nutrients include protein, iron, vitamin B12 and zinc. A vegan's diet may also lack calcium, riboflavin and vitamin D.

Protein

There are millions of different proteins – plant, animal and human. Like all proteins, food proteins are built from 'building blocks' called **amino acids**. Every cell in our body contains protein obtained from the food we eat and it is used throughout life for the growth, repair and maintenance of our bodies. There are more than twenty types of amino acids, but eight of them are essential in an adult's diet and nine are essential for children. These must be supplied by the foods we eat since they cannot be made in the body. Animal proteins such as meat, fish, eggs and milk contain all the essential amino acids in the right proportion which is why vegetarians must eat a varied diet that includes protein foods such as pulses, nuts and seeds.

Vegetarian products

Today's food industry has geared itself up to cater for its vegetarian consumers. A wide range of products can be purchased which meet a vegetarian's nutritional needs and many of these make use of **novel proteins** such as soya, myco-proteins (for example, Quorn™ which is made from a mushroom-like plant) and textured vegetable proteins. These products can be processed in a variety of ways to produce items such as tofu, soya milk and vegetarian readymeals and snacks.

allergic reactions

Reacting badly

Over the last two decades there has been a considerable growth of interest in adverse (bad) reactions to food, often called food allergy. In fact, only about 1–2 per cent of the population show an intolerance to food, although it is difficult to obtain accurate figures for the following reasons:

- an almost limitless number of foods and **additives** may cause reactions
- testing is very time consuming and some tests may not be particularly sensitive
- reactions vary between people and these can change over time, especially in children
- reactions to a food or additive may not show immediately.

Foods that have frequently been associated with food allergies include peanuts, wheat, cheese, wine, coffee, milk, eggs, potatoes, fish, oats and tomatoes.

adverse reactions that occur more than once and do not have **psychological** causes. The term 'food allergy' is used if a reaction is reproducible and involves an abnormal reaction in the immune system, resulting in **pathological** changes in the gut or elsewhere.

Allergic reactions can have an immediate or a delayed response. Symptoms might include redness of the skin, itching, swelling, breathing difficulties and abdominal pain. The severity of the symptoms varies between individuals but can range from mild to life-threatening such as **anaphylactic shock**. In 1999 about ten people in the UK died after going into anaphylactic shock following the consumption of what may have been the tiniest piece of nut. Anyone with a major allergic reaction needs to carry special adrenaline injections that they can administer themselves if necessary to reduce the symptoms.

Definitions

Various terms are used to describe allergic reactions to food, such as food intolerance, hypersensitivity and food allergy. Food intolerance and hypersensitivity are general terms for all

Anyone with coeliac disease must avoid a wide range of foods that contain gluten (a protein found in wheat, rye, barley and oats).

A wide range of food-related leaflets are produced by Foodsense. ▶

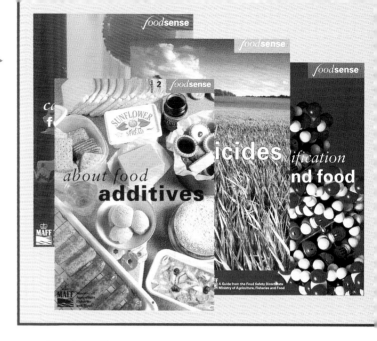

Coeliac disease

Coeliac disease is a condition which causes the wall of the small intestine to become damaged if gluten is eaten. Gluten is a protein found mainly in wheat but it is also present in rye, barley and oats. It is thought that around one in a thousand people in the UK suffer with coeliac disease.

If the lining of the small intestine becomes damaged the gut will fail to absorb adequate nutrients from food. As a result any of the following symptoms may occur: stomach pain, diarrhoea, vomiting, exhaustion, anaemia, bloating, mouth ulcers and weight loss. The only way a coeliac can prevent these symptoms is by avoiding all foods that contain gluten. Because gluten is present in flour, a common ingredient, a very wide range of foods are involved, including the majority of biscuits, cakes, pastries and breads, as well as products that have used a starch-based thickener such as many processed meals, desserts and snacks. Beer, too, has to be avoided as it cannot be guaranteed to be free from gluten.

Health food shops

Health food shops have sold products such as bread and cakes for coeliacs for some time but supermarkets and other stores are also beginning to cater for such specialist diets. Labelling is also being used to highlight gluten-free products.

Food additives

With the increase in food processing and manufactured products, additives are playing an increasing role in food production. Some consumer groups are opposed to their use because of the possibility of an adverse reaction. The additives most often mentioned in connection with sensitivity include colouring agents such as tartrazine (E102), found in some soft drinks, and antioxidants such as butylated hydroxytoluene (BHT), present in some margarines, and butylated hydroxyanisole (BHA), found in some soup mixes and cheese spreads.

Hyperactivity and children

Clearly it is difficult to link an allergy to an additive because they are not usually eaten on their own but there is concern that children who eat a lot of processed foods will be consuming a high proportion of additives in relation to body size. Some children suffer from increased activity, known as hyperactivity, after eating just a small amount of a food additive.

Certain additives, such as the sorbic acid found in some fruit yoghurts, are necessary to ensure that a food is preserved properly and is safe to eat. All additives given an 'E' number have been rigorously tested and are accepted as safe throughout the European Community.

13

diabetic diets

Glucose

Glucose is our body's main source of energy. The process of obtaining energy from food is complicated but most of our energy is supplied by carbohydrate foods such as bread, pasta, rice, potatoes and sugar. When all carbohydrates (except **NSP**) are eaten they are broken down during digestion and eventually absorbed as glucose, galactose and fructose. These **monosaccharides** then travel via the bloodstream to the liver (where galactose and fructose are converted to glucose) and the muscles.

The liver and muscles transform glucose into glycogen which acts as a reserve of carbohydrate for the body and can be converted back into glucose to supply the body with energy. Several hormones control the way in which our body uses glucose. One of these hormones is called insulin. Hormones are chemical messengers produced by one part of the body to cause a response in another part.

Insulin

Unfortunately for some people, the pancreas isn't always able to produce sufficient insulin and as a result the amount of glucose circulating in the blood is unusually large. Also, the liver and muscles fail to use the glucose for conversion to glycogen for energy. This means the body has to use fat and protein instead of carbohydrate foods as its source of energy which can be harmful. The result is a disease called diabetes mellitus.

Diabetes mellitus

Excessively high or low levels of glucose in the blood are very serious and must be controlled. Diabetics must be careful about what they eat and some have to take tablets or administer a daily injection of insulin. A diet high in complex carbohydrates and NSP (one containing wholemeal bread, wholegrain rice and cereals, vegetables and fruit) is recommended because these foods help to control the rate at which sugar is absorbed into the blood.

It is unclear exactly why diabetes develops or what causes it but people with diabetes do not make sufficient insulin in their bodies. There are two types of diabetes: young people's diabetes (or insulin dependent) and maturity onset diabetes (or non-insulin dependent).

Insulin-dependent diabetes usually develops suddenly and the symptoms are severe. It normally occurs before the age of forty and young people with this type of diabetes often have a **genetic** tendency towards it.

Non-insulin dependent diabetes does not require treatment with insulin because usually diabetics still produce some insulin of their own. They can control their diabetes by following healthy eating guidelines. This form tends to affect middle-aged and older people, although people who are overweight are at a higher risk of developing the disease as they get older.

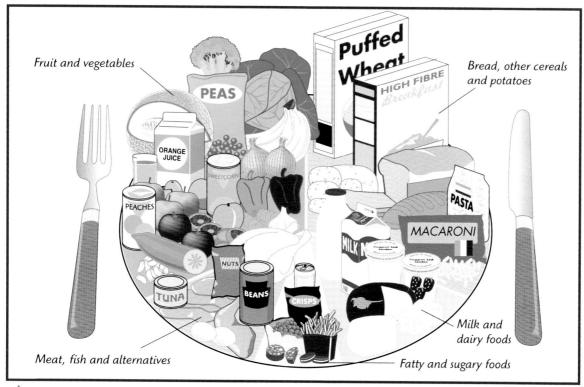

Fruit and vegetables

Bread, other cereals and potatoes

PEAS

Puffed Wheat

HIGH FIBRE Breakfast

ORANGE JUICE

SWEETCORN

PASTA

MACARONI

PEACHES

MILK

NUTS

TUNA

BEANS

CRISPS

Milk and dairy foods

Meat, fish and alternatives

Fatty and sugary foods

▲ A diet rich in complex carbohydrate foods, including NSP (non-starch polysaccharides) is advised for the management of diabetes. As recommended by the National Food Guide, fruit, vegetables, bread and other cereals form the largest portions of a healthy diet.

Healthy eating

Of course everyone is encouraged to follow a healthy eating regime and this is equally important for diabetics. The type of diet recommended for diabetics follows current views on healthy eating and so includes reduced fat intake, especially **saturated fat**, reduced salt and sugar intake but increased NSP intake. Of course, it can be difficult to monitor the diet of a young child so it is important that children understand the need to stick to their diet.

A diabetic must ensure that they do not have too much sugar or sugary products, such as sweets, cakes, biscuits and fizzy drinks, which cause a rapid rise in blood sugar levels. However, although the amount needs to be reduced, they do not have to be avoided altogether. Sweet treats can be eaten occasionally, preferably after a meal rather than on an empty stomach. It is now generally thought that products such as diabetic chocolate are not necessary because they are often no lower in fat or **calories** than ordinary chocolate.

Diabetic guidelines

As well as following a healthy diet, diabetics also need to consider how much and how often they eat. It is important to eat regular meals and to avoid skipping meals. They must watch out for hidden fats that are found in pastries, cakes, biscuits and snacks. Alcohol consumption should be kept to a minimum and should not be used to replace meals. Drink must not be consumed on an empty stomach as it lowers blood sugar levels. Weight needs to be monitored to avoid becoming overweight.

multicultural matters

Consumer influence

The consumer is a powerful force behind the development of new food products. If the majority of consumers started showing concern about their salt intake, then manufacturers would gradually reduce the levels of salt in processed foods. This is equally true when it comes to meeting the needs of different consumer groups. For example, 'meals for one' have helped to fill a gap in the market for the growing number of adults living on their own. As society has become more multicultural, so the demand for foods traditionally from other cultures has increased. In the UK, one person in fifteen is from an ethnic minority group.

Multicultural societies

All cultures have customs with which they are traditionally associated,

▼ *In the UK there is growing interest in foods from other cultures. People are more receptive to different ingredients, flavours, aromas and methods of cooking.*

although not all members of that culture necessarily follow them. Dietary customs are often associated with religious beliefs such as the Christian tradition of eating pancakes on Shrove Tuesday (the day before Lent). During the **fasting** of Lent, eggs are forbidden so they are used up in the pancake batter. Ramadan takes place during the ninth month of the Muslim year when Muslims are expected to fast during daylight hours.

In the Asian community there are many regional and religious variations but generally **staple** foods include chapattis (Indian unleavened bread) and rice. Pulses are used quite extensively, especially by vegetarians, for example in dahl (an Indian dish made from lentils). Muslims do not eat pork and all meat must be halal which means it has been slaughtered according to Muslim law by a halal butcher. Hindus and Sikhs do not eat beef or drink alcohol. Many Hindus are vegetarian as they are against violence and, for them, the cow is sacred.

Barbecued food is popular in hot climates such as Australia.

Within the Jewish community, meat must be kosher which means it is slaughtered according to Jewish law. Followers of Judaism do not eat pork or shellfish. Also, a three-hour gap must pass between eating meat and dairy products and even the preparation of these foods must take place separately, so different sinks and equipment are required.

The diet of the Afro-Caribbean community is often based on rice and maize (corn) as well as vegetables such as yams, sweet potatoes and plantains. These foods all have a high starch content, so form the staple diet. Both meat and fish are eaten although Rastafarians are vegetarian and avoid all processed and preserved foods as well as dairy products, eggs, salt and alcohol.

Further afield

Of course, the demand for foods with a multicultural feel does not just come from people who have their roots in another culture. Generally, people are travelling more than ever before and are visiting a wider variety of countries. By visiting countries and getting a taste of another culture, people later want to replicate those dishes for themselves at home or buy them in a restaurant or shop. This has resulted in an increase in the variety of restaurants as well as the range of food products on sale. People are also more receptive to new ideas and are prepared to try dishes from other countries.

Methods of cooking

Along with an interest in different ingredients, flavours and aromas, new dishes introduce the opportunity for new methods of cooking. Indian cuisine uses the tandoor oven, oriental food is cooked in a wok, a tagine is used in Moroccan cookery and barbecued food is popular in hot climates such as in Australia.

In fact, despite the unpredictability of the weather, barbecues are becoming increasingly trendy in cooler climates such as in Western Europe, and not just to entertain the family at weekends. *Elle* magazine has provided a catwalk barbecue on the Thames and chef Nigel Tunicliffe has started a catering company called Blistering Barbecues to whet the appetite of outdoor eaters.

Project

It is thought that Australian cuisine is going to be the next big culinary influence in Europe. Investigate ingredients native to Australia and dishes that are popular with Australians. Then design and make a family meal that has an Australian influence but would be popular with families in Europe. Give your new dish a suitable name.

from sandwich to sushi

Fast food

When you think of fast food you don't necessarily think of a sandwich, although sandwiches are both quick to prepare and easy to eat. Like all fast food, you don't have to go to the trouble of making sandwiches yourself as they can now be purchased in all sorts of retail outlets, from supermarkets to petrol stations. In fact, sandwiches are now the most popular convenience food. Consumers spend more on ready-made sandwiches than any other fast food. The British sandwich market is currently worth £3.5 billion – that's over three times more than the burger and pizza markets.

The sandwich is thought to have been invented by the 4th Earl of Sandwich in the 18th century. If the Earl had chosen to use one of the many titles he was offered, we could have been eating a 'Portsmouth' today! According to the British Sandwich Association, there are approximately 2.2 billion sandwiches eaten every year in the UK alone (this figure includes all bread filled snacks such as pittas and rolls). In fact, the sandwich industry is so big in the UK that it provides full and part-time employment for around 320,000 people.

Varieties of sandwich

Sandwiches are perfect when it comes to refuelling during a hectic lunchtime. They are easily transportable and can contain a variety of different fillings; they also satisfy the appetite quickly and can be relatively nutritious. Of course, consumer demand has led to many variations on the original theme.

The 4th Earl of Sandwich would be impressed – the British sandwich market is worth three times more than the pizza and burger markets.

For example, the bread may be wholewheat, wholegrain, rye or granary, it may be flavoured with cheese or coloured with the addition of red pepper or tomato. Fillings have become both adventurous, such as Wensleydale cheese and watercress with carrot chutney, and decidedly challenging, such as sausage and egg in baked bean bread!

A further expansion of the sandwich has been the introduction of items such as tortilla wraps and filled Italian ciabatta bread. While these may be slightly more expensive than the average sandwich, it would appear that although people have less time for eating they are often prepared to spend a little more on the food they consume. The convenience of prepacked food is also tempting, especially when an entire packed lunch can be picked up at the local shop. Sandwiches are teamed up with crisps, a drink and perhaps a piece of fruit or yoghurt for a complete lunchtime experience without any effort.

Bagels

Another popular bread-based lunchtime snack is the bagel. Originally from America, the bagel looks a bit like a doughnut without the sugar coating and has a denser texture. One of the bagel's selling points is that it is low in fat (although the nutritional information shows this doesn't necessarily mean it is low in **calories**). Bagels are available in a variety of sweet and savoury flavours, in addition to the plain version. They can be eaten hot or cold, filled or unfilled. After toasting they may be spread with all kinds of fillings from soft cheese to peanut butter.

According to a bagel company called Oi! Bagel, the most popular flavours with their customers include poppy seed bagel with smoked salmon and cream cheese, sesame seed bagel with bacon and cream cheese and onion bagel with tuna salad and lemon.

Sushi

The latest competition to sandwiches is sushi, a Japanese dish containing rice and sushi vinegar. These oriental snacks have now found their way out of restaurants or sushi bars and onto the high street as an exciting new lunchtime snack. Sushi comes in bite-sized pieces and, in addition to cooked rice, can contain fish, seafood, egg and nori seaweed. The ingredients are carefully layered, then rolled up before being sliced and up-ended ready to be served.

Although sushi can be manufactured quite easily these days, in Japan it traditionally took a chef about ten years to learn the art of sushi-making. The slicing of the raw ingredients requires a great deal of knife skill and the quantity of each ingredient must be precisely judged in order to obtain the perfect result. The sushi is traditionally rolled on bamboo mats and requires just the right amount of pressure.

▼ *Japanese sushi is now a popular lunchtime snack.*

too much, too little

Food as fuel

Eating should be fun but for many people food can cause unnecessary suffering. This may be because a poor diet has led to health problems in later life or it may be that food is eaten, or avoided, for emotional rather than physical reasons.

Food is a fuel and that is how most animals would view it. However, for humans, food comes from a wide variety of sources which can be combined and cooked in numerous ways, making eating much more interesting than a simple refuelling process. Also, because humans are complex and sociable beings, in addition to our physical wellbeing, eating can affect our **psychological** and emotional state.

Anorexia nervosa

Anorexia nervosa is a disorder which makes people obsessively anxious about their body weight. The name is in fact confusing because 'anorexia' literally means 'loss of appetite' but people with anorexia nervosa do not lose their appetite. Instead, they become so frightened of gaining weight that they eat as little as possible. It is thought that anorexia affects about 1 per cent of women between the ages of 15 and 30 in the UK. However, a small number of young men are also affected and anorexia nervosa is becoming an increasing problem in girls under 15.

Many people believe the media and fashion industries contribute to the high incidence of anorexia nervosa in the Western world. For many years the way women have been portrayed by these industries has been as someone who is very slim. These images can influence teenage girls whose bodies are changing as they develop into women. Many girls feel they must diet in order to maintain or achieve a slim figure but this may well be to the detriment of their health. Fortunately there is now a slight move by the media towards using models with more realistic proportions.

For the anorexic, the fear of fatness goes far beyond a simple desire to be slim. For them, the need to make themselves thinner dominates all other emotions. Even when they are very underweight they may still see themselves as fat. This distorted perception of how they look is characteristic of the disorder. Anorexics feel that their value as a person is directly affected by their body shape.

Bulimia nervosa

Bulimia nervosa is also a disorder whereby someone is unable to relate normally to food but in this case they do not generally have the dramatic weight loss associated with anorexia nervosa. A bulimic usually swings between the frantic activity of bingeing, then follows this with an urgent desire to get rid of everything that has been consumed. The bingeing of food is almost always carried out in secret and may involve eating absolutely anything that is available and edible (although uncooked foods may also be chosen as part of the binge). After eating such a large amount, someone with bulimia nervosa will then panic and need to rid their body of

everything they have consumed. This may be done by making themselves vomit or they may take laxatives (to stimulate the bowels) or diuretics (to increase the excretion of urine), or even use all three. Alternatively, excessive **fasting** or exercise may be undertaken to compensate for the high **calorie** intake. Initially, someone with bulimia nervosa may feel they have found a way to control their lives because they can eat whatever they like without putting on any weight. However, in reality it is the bulimia nervosa that actually has the control and dictates the way in which a person lives their life. Just like anorexia nervosa, the incidence of bulimia is more common among women and both conditions can have serious medical consequences, as shown below.

Anorexia nervosa	Bulimia nervosa
• Poor circulation	• Tooth decay
• Low blood pressure	• Irregular periods
• Brittle bones	• Damage to the bowel
• Increased facial hair	• Constipation
• Loss of periods/ infertility	• Heart and kidney disease
• Fainting and dizziness	• Intestinal damage
• Hair loss	• Puffiness of face and fingers
• Dehydration	• Increased hair growth on face and body
• Kidney damage	• Mineral imbalances in the body

Endorphin boost

The American Nobel prize-winning scientist, James Watson, has a different theory about body size. Instead of seeing thinness as something to desire, he suggests that a lack of body fat can make people discontent. After studying body chemicals he believes that extra body fat leads to a boost of endorphins, the natural mood-enhancing chemical. The more fat, the more endorphins and so the more content a person feels.

addicted to food

Obesity

In 1999 the UK government laid down targets for improving the nation's health. One of these targets was to reduce the incidence of **coronary heart disease**. One of the many **risk factors** known to increase a person's chance of developing coronary heart disease is obesity.

Obesity officially became a disease around 50 years ago when it entered the International Classification of Diseases. It can be defined according to a body mass index (BMI). A person's BMI is calculated by dividing their weight in kilograms (kg) by their height in metres squared (m^2). The resulting figure can then be checked against the following BMI categories:

BMI	Grade
<20	Underweight
20–25	Normal weight
25–30	Overweight
>30	Obese

Knowledge of this system is important for those concerned about their health because, in general, risks begin to increase when the BMI is above 25. The risks increase even more rapidly when a BMI of over 30 is reached. However, care must be taken when using such a system as it does not take account of the components of body weight. Muscle, for example, is heavier than fat, so a trained athlete may be classified as obese despite having very little body fat!

Fat versus lean

Clearly, the amount of body fat is an important aspect of health, particularly in relation to coronary heart disease. For women, the proportion of fat on their body tends to be higher than that of men, due to their reproductive role and hormone activity. As a guide, an adult woman should have between 25 and 28 per cent body fat whereas an adult male should have 15 per cent.

The high fat content of the typical Western diet is partly responsible for the increase in body fat levels over the last decade. People tend to snack rather than eat whole meals, relying on fast foods such as takeaways. A high proportion of these foods, such as chips, burgers, fried chicken and doughnuts, are fried or contain a great deal of fat. In 1999 there were 2000 more takeaways and restaurants operating in the UK than in 1996.

However, the food industry can't be entirely to blame for an increase in obesity, after all, the industry claims to only give consumers what they want. Other lifestyle habits that are likely to contribute include spending more time sitting down and lack of exercise. Occupations are generally less physical than they used to be and more people travel by car, even for short journeys. Fewer children walk to and from school and the increase in home computers has meant that it is not just a television screen that captivates young and old alike during the evenings.

▲ A diet high in fat contributes to today's obesity problem. Reducing calorie intake and exercising can help.

The consequences of becoming overweight make grim reading. Statistics show that obese people are both more likely to die prematurely and more likely to develop diabetes.

Slimming down

The amount of people with excess weight today makes little sense when supermarket shelves are packed with low-fat, reduced **calorie** foods and drinks. Despite these products, and the medical evidence stating the consequences of obesity, it remains exceedingly difficult for people to lose weight. A person really has to want to reduce the amount they eat in order to achieve a significant difference in their weight. Slimming clubs and classes are usually very helpful, mainly due to the support offered by other people. Also, foods are often classified, perhaps using a points system, so it is easier to decide what to eat, how much and how often.

Any diet offering a great deal of weight loss in a short period of time must be

Fat cats

Unfortunately, it is not just people who are being classified as obese. In 1997 a survey of pets showed that 14 per cent of cats and 15 per cent of dogs in the UK are clinically obese. In fact, three-quarters of dogs in the UK were defined as overweight, making them the fattest dogs in Europe.

regarded with caution. It is likely that any weight lost will go straight back on after the diet has stopped. Diets like these cannot be followed long term because they do not supply all the necessary nutrients. For serious obesity (BMI of 40+) surgery may be an option if all else has failed. This can involve stapling the stomach so that only small amounts of food can be eaten. Food supplements are likely to be needed afterwards and plastic surgery may be necessary to remove surplus folds of skin after the weight has been lost. This really is a last resort.

Food or nutrient?

Most people do not think about nutrients when they eat food. However, our diet can contibute to the risk of diseases such as **coronary heart disease**, so in order to help people choose a diet that contains the foods they need for good health, dietary guidelines have been drawn up by various health organizations. Dietary guidelines do not tell people exactly what to eat because there are many healthy diets. Individuals must choose a diet according to their own lifestyle and preferences.

In the UK, the Ministry of Agriculture, Fisheries and Food (MAFF) produced *Eight Guidelines for a Healthy Diet* in 1990. These were intended to be an update on diet and health for people with some knowledge of nutrition and to give guidance on *The Balance of Good Health Guide* (see below).

Eight Guidelines for a Healthy Diet

1. Enjoy your food.
2. Eat a variety of different foods.
3. Eat the right amount to be a healthy weight.
4. Eat plenty of foods rich in starch and fibre.
5. Don't eat too much fat.
6. Don't eat sugary foods too often.
7. Look after the vitamins and minerals in your food.
8. If you drink, keep within sensible limits.

Current dietary guidelines

A number of organizations have put forward dietary guidelines over recent years. For example, *The National Food Guide: The Balance of Good Health* was published by the Health Education Authority in 1994 (see page 15). Although the guide applies to most people, it is not suitable for very young children, for some people under medical supervision or for those who have special dietary requirements. However, it can be used by individual consumers, food producers, manufacturers and caterers.

An advantage of having a guide such as this is that it gives a consistent message about eating. In fact, the types of food we are being advised to eat now are very similar to recommendations in previous years. The aim of the guide is to help get the right advice to everyone. It is reinforced with campaigns such as the 'Eat 5' campaign that encourages people to eat at least five portions of fruit and vegetables every day.

DRVs

In 1991 a British government committee called the Committee on Medical Aspects of Food Policy (COMA) published a report entitled 'Dietary Reference Values'. It contained details of the amounts of the various nutrients we need to consume. The report provides details of the range of nutrient requirements likely to be found in the UK population. A very wide range of vitamins and minerals are included and recommendations for the amount of fat, carbohydrate and **NSP** (non-starch polysaccharide) are included.

▲ The 'Eat 5' campaign encourages people to eat at least five portions of fruit and vegetables every day.

DRVs for the energy-providing nutrients

- Fat should supply 35% of total energy, with no more than 11% coming from **saturated fat**
- Protein should supply 15% of total energy
- Carbohydrate should supply 50% of total energy (39% from starch, 11% from non-milk extrinsic sugar, i.e. all types of sugar, syrup and honey)

The Dietary Reference Values (DRVs) can be used for the following purposes:
- to assess the adequacy of diets of individuals and groups of people
- to calculate the nutritional content of meals and menus
- to plan food supplies.

However, the DRV report was not very 'user friendly' for the general public, and this was why *The Balance of Good Health* guide was introduced.

Government guidelines

In 1999 the British government published a white paper concerned with the nation's health. The government declared that 'good health, like good education, should be within reach of all'. The white paper, entitled, 'Saving Lives: Our Healthier Nation' had two goals:
- to improve the health of the population as a whole by increasing the length of people's lives and the number of years people spend free from illness
- to improve the health of those with a low income and to narrow the health gap.

These goals are consistent with the aims of both the World Health Organization (Europe) and the European Community (EC).

healthy eats

New launch

In August 2000, the international high street store Marks and Spencer launched a range of healthy foods for kids. Labelled 'Everyday Eating' the products were developed specifically for children aged three to eight years old and the range consists of meals containing protein and vegetables, snack foods, desserts, fruits and vegetables. The reason these types of foods have been chosen is because they represent all the elements of a balanced diet.

Cordon bleu

The Marks and Spencer range may appeal to parents because it has been developed with the help of Annabel Karmel, a well-known author and trained cordon bleu chef. Annabel Karmel has written several books about cooking for children and acted as a consultant to Marks and Spencer during the development of their new range of foods. She provided recipe ideas and expertise on creating healthy food that children would want to eat. Generally, children do not choose foods because they are healthy and are more likely to go for foods that are sweet or high in fat or foods that are popular with their friends. Young children are strongly influenced by their **peer group** when it comes to food.

Kiddie tactics

To make the new range appealing to children, the Product Development Team came up with foods that were colourful, fun and often tactile. For example, one product called Fajitas (which includes lean chicken, peppers, cheese, salsa and sour cream) has to be assembled by the children as they are eating it. Children often enjoy this 'hands on' approach to eating and (as long as the 'hands on' method is appropriate) it is an effective way of getting children to eat healthy foods.

The range also uses entertaining names such as Tomatoes with Hidden Vegetable Sauce and Make a Face Fruit Salad. To entice fussy eaters, there are also mini versions of some of the dishes so they are not put off by having to eat a large portion. All recipes developed during the making of the 'Everyday Eating' range have been tested by a panel of youngsters, including Annabel Karmel's three children.

Product range

Titles from Marks and Spencer's 'Everyday Eating' range include:

Chicken Noodles
'These noodles are oodles of fun but not too long so they're easy to eat.'

Cheesy Spirals
'Want to make eating fun? Give these delicious spirals a whirl.'

Shepherds Pie
'Want to make them smile? Try this "happy face" family favourite.'

10 Sea Giants
'Whales? Sharks? Just the best of the catch.'

Fromage Frais
'Thank goodness, no bits, just smooth, creamy and totally delicious.'

◀ *Marks and Spencer 'Everyday Eating' foods come with a pledge to parents: 'a balanced diet for healthy, happy kids approved by a team of experts, enjoyed by a panel of children'.*

Designing for children

Getting young children to eat healthy foods can be very difficult. Imagine you have been asked by another big food producer to develop a range of healthy meals for children between the ages of 5 and 10. Your range must include both sweet and savoury meals and all must include a healthy balance of nutrients. It is important to find out what children like to eat first, so try asking a group of young children about different ingredients. Also, ask them how they like to eat (for example with a fork, spoon or their fingers). Present your ideas as coloured design ideas with explanatory labels and notes.

Parent-friendly

There is currently a lot of consumer concern about the use of **additives** in food products so the 'Everyday Eating' range has been produced without any artificial preservatives, colours or flavours. Some of the dishes are ready to eat while others only require simple preparation so they will appeal to busy parents. Many of the products can also be microwaved.

Dietary guidelines

Until recently, dietary guidelines given on food labels only referred to adult intakes. However, Marks and Spencer have also introduced daily nutritional guidelines for children. These guidelines were developed with a nutritional consultant and detail the recommended daily intake of **calories** (kilojoules), fat and salt suitable for children aged three to six. Products in the 'Everyday Eating' range have a tick panel so that parents can identify at a glance the key nutritional details of each product.

The children's range includes some treats and party foods but these are packaged differently and are in a different location in the store.

▲ *Marks and Spencer market their 'Everyday Eating' range specifically at children and emphasize the notion that healthy eating can be fun.*

Pregnancy

Evidence provided by studies of pregnant women and their babies has shown that if a woman can adapt her diet (as necessary) before conceiving, then there are fewer health risks for the baby. What a woman eats and drinks three to six months before conception and for the first few weeks of pregnancy is thought to greatly influence the early development of the embryo.

Recommendations include a daily supply of the B vitamin folic acid (known as folate in its natural form), to be taken from the time contraception is stopped until the twelfth week of pregnancy. This is believed to significantly reduce the risk of giving birth to a baby with a congenital neural tube defect such as spina bifida (in which the spine has not developed properly). Foods that contain folate include brussels sprouts, spinach, granary bread, nuts and oranges, as well as various **fortified** breakfast cereals and breads, but daily supplements of folic

acid are recommended because even a healthy diet is unlikely to supply the amount required. (Liver also contains folate, but due to the high levels of vitamin A in liver, women who are pregnant or are thinking of becoming pregnant, should avoid liver altogether as high levels of vitamin A have been linked with birth defects.)

Alcohol

An excessive intake of alcohol could lead to birth defects so it is best avoided before conception and preferably for the first twelve weeks of pregnancy. However, after that less than one unit a day is not considered to be a risk.

1 unit of alcohol =

- half a pint of ordinary strength (3.5% ABV) lager/beer/cider
- 1 small glass of wine (9% ABV) Note: many wines are 11 or 12% ABV
- 1 x 25ml measure of spirit (40% ABV)

Planning a menu

By following current dietary guidelines and eating sensible amounts of food, a pregnant woman can achieve a healthy, balanced diet. Towards the end of pregnancy (in the last **trimester**) a woman may need to increase her **calorie** intake by about 200 calories (0.8MJ) per day. Suggest a week's menu for each of the following stages of pregnancy; one month; six months and eight months. Remember to include a variety of foods!

Infants

A human baby is able to survive on milk alone for its first three months. The milk may be breast milk or formula milk specially developed for babies. Once a baby reaches its fourth month it can cope with a rusk or cereal mixed with milk. When it reaches five or six months it can start to bite and chew lumps of food and this is the stage when an increased variety of tastes and textures can be introduced in the diet. The process of introducing foods other than milk to the baby's diet is known as weaning.

It is especially important for pregnant women and women who are breastfeeding, and babies and toddlers, to avoid infection from food. Infants have an immature immune system so cannot fight infection easily. Food should be hygienically prepared and cooked or reheated thoroughly. Ingredients must be fresh and well within their datemark.

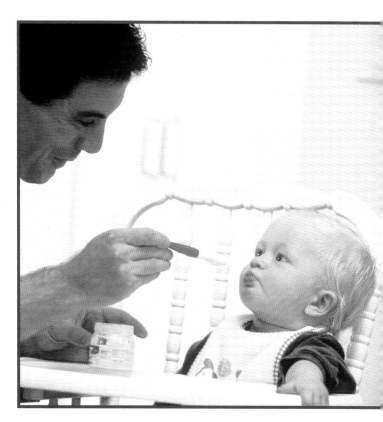

If a baby has the same food as the rest of the family (even if mashed or puréed) the food should contain no added salt. This is because a baby's kidneys cannot cope with additional salt. Adults can sprinkle salt on their own meals later or perhaps they will be encouraged to cut down on their salt intake!

It is also important to help a child develop good dietary habits during its first few years. By not adding sugar to foods and avoiding sugary drinks, a child is less likely to get a taste for sweet things. Even teeth buried beneath the gums can suffer tooth decay. The more varied and interesting food can be made for young children, the more likely they are to be adventurous in their tastes as they grow up.

Young people

After their first year, the growth rate of young children is not as great. It tends to occur in spurts which are often accompanied by surges of appetite. Activity increases during the second year as a child becomes increasingly mobile but the amount a young child can eat remains small due to a limited capacity. Having a full set of milk teeth by the age of about two also increases the variety of foods they can eat. For both these reasons, healthy snacks between meals are important for additional energy and for a wider range of food experiences. In 1995 research was carried out in the UK by the National Diet and Nutrition

Healthy snack ideas for young children

- sandwiches containing cucumber, savoury spreads, chopped tomato with cheese
- fresh or dried fruit
- raw vegetables cut into pieces
- dry breakfast cereal
- savoury biscuits
- yoghurt or milk
- plain popcorn
- cheesy scones

Survey. The survey showed that, on the whole, children were eating large amounts of salt and sugar and insufficient fruit and vegetables. Children were also considered to be receiving inadequate levels of iron. These aspects of every young child's diet should be given special attention.

Kitchen gadgets

At one time, new food-related technological developments were mainly based around the domestic kitchen, with food processors, automatic ovens, electric whisks, fridge-freezers, microwave ovens and so on. Today, new kitchen gadgets, such as the bread-maker, still appear from time to time but the main thrust of new technology has been in the food industry itself.

Towards the end of the 1990s innovations in food and packaging appeared at a phenomenal rate. Once the microwave oven was well-established in the majority of homes, food technologists were frantically developing products that could be reheated (still in its packaging) within minutes. For example, readymeals, can now be reheated from the chilled, frozen or **ambient** state. Even the traditionally fat-laden chip was given a high-tech 'healthy' image by being packaged in a box ready for a blast of microwaves.

Novel pizza

Of course, developments such as these do not happen overnight. Adequate market research must be carried out to ensure this is what the consumer wants. Also, a new food product must go through a number of tests in order to produce a quality result that meets the relevant food safety requirements. For example, pizzas are now commonplace. The pizza range has been extended by adapting the texture, thickness and flavour of the base. A variety of ingredients are used as toppings and the pizzas have been folded, rolled, divided and shaped in order to produce something different. But, just when the consumer thought nothing new could come from a pizza, along came a pizza that can be cooked from frozen in a toaster without its topping being lost!

Value-added

Products such as the toasted pizza and many other convenience foods have led to the term 'value-added'. This refers to foods that have undergone secondary processing in order to produce ready-to-use products. Consider the difference in effort involved in making a hot rice pudding using ingredients and heating ready-made puddings.

Homemade rice pudding
Method: Place pudding rice in dish with milk, sugar, butter and nutmeg. Bake for $2\frac{1}{2}$ hours, stirring 2–3 times during cooking.

Tinned rice pudding
Method: Empty contents of can into saucepan. Heat gently for 3–4 minutes, stirring frequently.

Ambient rice pudding
Method: Remove all foil. Heat on full power (650w microwave) for 50 seconds, stirring halfway through heating time.

Functional foods

As well as demanding high-quality foods that require little effort at home, today's consumer also wants 'healthy' products.

Definitions of healthy are likely to vary depending on whether you are talking to a consumer, a manufacturer or a nutritionist, but nevertheless, a vast array of products have some sort of health label.

Once again, technology has played a significant role in the development of foods that are acceptable to consumers and yet are low in fat, sugar or salt, or high in **NSP**. Foods which claim to have specific health benefits are often referred to as functional foods. Any food that makes a specific health claim should obtain a licence under the Medicines Act so it is wise for a consumer to check this out before relying on the claim. In addition, it is worth reading the nutritional labelling of any product with a health claim. Unlike other foods, a nutritional breakdown is required to be on the label by law.

Benecol®

Benecol® foods are described as functional foods because they claim to lower blood **cholesterol** when eaten as part of a healthy diet. Cholesterol is a fatty substance naturally present in the

▲ *These products are referred to as 'value-added' because they have undergone secondary processing which provides the consumer with a ready-to-use product.*

body. If levels in the blood become too high, the cholesterol can contribute to the 'clogging up' of the arteries which could increase the risk of **coronary heart disease**.

Benecol® products, such as a margarine spread and yoghurt, contain plant stanol **esters** which occur naturally in plants such as corn, beans and rye. As they were known to have the ability to lower cholesterol, a Finnish food manufacturer called Raisio, in the 1990s, managed to invent and **patent** a process of blending the plant stanols with rapeseed oil to create plant stanol esters. It is believed that when the recommended amount of plant stanol ester is introduced into the diet the amount of cholesterol absorbed from food falls from 50 to 20 per cent. However, it is important to remember that blood cholesterol levels and the body's response to dietary levels also depends on a person's **genetic** make-up.

packing food

Packing up

Packaging has become big business in the Western world. There are few items of food without at least one layer of wrapping. Even if you do manage to reach the supermarket checkout with a package-free product, the chances are the cashier will put it into a plastic bag for you anyway! This extra packaging does not just result in mountains of waste plastic, paper and cardboard for the consumer; manufacturers are having to shoulder the burden, too. The cost of packaging materials is rising at a higher rate than the food itself. But for the manufacturer, it is worth the investment. Packaging is believed to have a greater influence on food sales than something as important as the quality of the food inside.

Packaging costs

Food packaging usually ends up in a bin. In fact, packaging makes up about 30 per cent of the UK's domestic waste. Every household adds to the country's 20-million-tonne rubbish mountain by throwing away, on average, a tonne of waste each year. While consumers are paying for all the packaging, it is the environment that is suffering the consequences. It has been estimated that for every £75 spent on groceries, £10 pays for the packaging. For certain products, packaging costs are staggeringly high, for example a box of breakfast cereal can cost 45 times more than the price a farmer gets for its main ingredient.

The increase in the amount of packaging used today has significant consequences for us and our environment, including:

- extra costs due to the collection and disposal of the extra waste and the subsequent pollution created by that waste
- increased production of materials to meet the demand for packaging, and increased waste products as a result
- loss of natural resources such as trees (paper, cardboard) and oil (plastics).

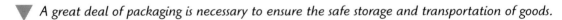

▼ *A great deal of packaging is necessary to ensure the safe storage and transportation of goods.*

Packaging can enhance the aesthetic appeal of a product but is it really necessary?

Recycling

There are many ways in which consumers, retailers and manufacturers can help to reduce the amount of waste generated by food packaging. Many materials are now successfully recycled by being made into new products or by being reused. Recycling bins are located at many supermarkets and household refuse sites. Here, consumers can drop off used plastic bottles, glass bottles, aluminium and steel cans. The materials are then collected by recycling companies or local councils and then taken to be cleaned and processed for reuse. There is always more that could be done, of course. In German supermarkets separate bins are provided next to the checkout so the extra plastic packaging can be removed before the goods are even taken home.

Unfortunately, the latest marketing trend of 'buy one get one free' (known as 'bogof' in the trade!) encourages extra packaging, for example plastic film around several items such as cans. Children's items also tend to command extra packaging, perhaps to encourage them (or their parents) to buy the goods.

Why pack?

Packaging does, of course, have an important role to play for the following reasons. Packaging:

- is an integral part of the food processing chain, helping manufacturers and consumers transport, store, sell/purchase and use foods more efficiently
- provides protection from external damage and contamination during distribution and keeps the food in good condition throughout its shelf-life
- communicates all necessary information to the consumer about the food, including certain aspects required by law
- is a means of ensuring products are delivered in measured quantities and in the expected condition
- can make food look more attractive which can promote its use and increase sales.

It is important for a manufacturer to choose carefully when packaging food products. In addition to practical factors such as the type of food product, the choice of packaging will also depend on other **aesthetic** factors. A soft drink, for example, could be sold in a plastic bottle but if the image of this drink is one of an 'upmarket' beverage, a glass bottle may be more appropriate. This would have the added advantage of being suitable for recycling.

Packing in layers

Packaging used for food products can be divided into three groups:

Primary packaging – the layer that contains the food product, for example a plastic yoghurt carton

Secondary packaging – used when several food products are packed together, for example a cardboard sleeve that holds four yoghurt pots together

Transit packaging – for transporting and distributing large quantities of a food product to retailers, for example many packs of four yoghurts are placed in large containers, usually cardboard boxes to help with the handling, storage and transportation of the goods.

Glass

Glass has been used as a form of packaging for centuries. Although it is breakable and heavy to transport, these disadvantages are often felt to be outweighed by its ability to be recycled. Glass is easy to wash and sterilize so it can be recycled many times. It does not affect or react with its contents and it can be clear so consumers can see what they are buying. It can also be made into different shapes and sizes. From the manufacturer's point of view, glass is relatively cheap to produce because it can be made quickly using a highly automated production line (a system that uses machines to carry out tasks automatically). Glass can withstand high temperatures so it is suitable for use with products that are to be processed by sterilization and preservation, such as jams and pickles. Glass is useful for fizzy drinks because it can resist the internal pressure created by the gas.

▲ Glass bottles are an example of primary packaging.

Metal

Steel or aluminium cans are used to preserve and contain a whole range of foods from fruit to frankfurters. Metal is also used to create foil containers, lids and sheets, and metallic finishes are sometimes applied to other materials such as plastics.

Steel cans have to be coated with a layer of tin to prevent the steel from rusting and they do not have 'ring-pulls' because these are easier to make in aluminium. As steel contains more than one metal it is more difficult to recycle. Aluminium, on the other hand, is a strong, lightweight material that is expensive to produce so it is important that it is recycled. Cans are either made from one continuous piece of metal or they are made with a seam. They can withstand high temperatures, and canned food has a shelf-life of many months. Aluminium foil trays and containers have the advantage of being pliable and they can be reused as well as recycled.

Paper

Cardboard and paper are made from cellulose (plant material) and wood pulp. These are natural materials so it is important that all packaging made from them is recycled. Paper and card packaging often has additional layers in order to improve its strength. Plastic or wax coatings are used on card containers and corrugated cardboard is often used for boxes to make them better insulators. Many food products now have cardboard sleeves on which labelling information can be displayed.

Plastic

Plastic first became popular as a food packaging material in the 1960s. It has the advantages of being reasonably cheap and easy to produce, very versatile and extremely lightweight. However, some plastics are felt to be unsuitable for use due to the presence of certain chemicals which can **leach out** into foods, particularly those high in fats.

Most food packaging is thermoplastic which means it becomes soft on heating and hardens once cool. The advantage of this is that it can be shaped while soft and will stay in that shape unless it is reheated. A variety of different plastics are used for packaging food and are known by abbreviations:

- PP (polypropylene) is used as a clear film or moulded to produce a rigid container.
- PET (polyester) is also used as a film or for moulding into containers but as it can withstand very high temperatures it can be used for products that need to be reheated in a microwave.
- PVC (polyvinylchloride) is only used for a limited amount of food packaging due to its possible toxicity in combination with some foods. It is heat resistant and **permeable** to gas and water.
- PS (polystyrene) is used when food needs extra protection. It is a good insulator, too, so it is often used for takeaway food such as burgers.

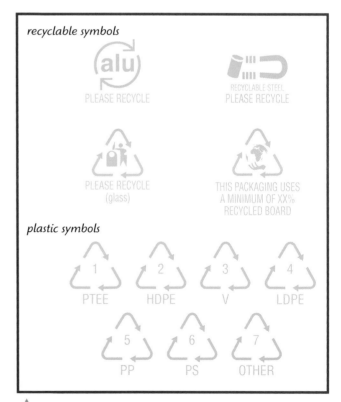

▲ Look out for recycling symbols on food packaging.

MAP

Preserving packaging

Preservation helps to delay food spoiling. Packaging enables food to be protected from external damage. **Modified atmosphere packaging (MAP)** provides a way of preserving food through the process of packaging and is sometimes referred to as a shelf-life extension technique.

MAP is packaging that contains food in an atmosphere that is different to the Earth's normal atmosphere (the air we breathe). MAP usually involves the use of three gases: carbon dioxide, nitrogen and oxygen. Different foods are packaged with different combinations and quantities of these gases, depending on the food type.

> The Earth's atmosphere consists of:
>
> - Nitrogen (N) 78.1%
> - Oxygen (O_2) 20.96%
> - Carbon dioxide (CO_2) 0.34%
> - plus trace inert gases (gases that do not normally react with other materials) and water vapour

Extending shelf-life

The introduction of the MAP techniques has meant that the shelf-life of various products can be extended by between 50 and 500 per cent. This is a bonus for both consumers and retailers because waste is minimized. Retailers can also be more flexible when restocking and ordering their goods. Another advantage is that by using MAP there is less need for the artificial preservatives that are so unpopular with consumers.

How does it work?

Of course, no food product can last forever. Food spoilage is a natural phenomenon although the rate at which different foods decay depends on the type of food and the conditions in which it is kept. Fresh meat and fish and dairy products such as milk, cheese and cream are all regarded as highly perishable. This means they only have a relatively short shelf-life.

The fresh meat sold in a supermarket may be packaged using a MAP technique. This enables it to stay on the shelf for longer both in the shop and at home. A second advantage is that the colour of the meat is maintained for longer. The appearance of food is very important to consumers and it is also a good indicator of quality. MAP can involve a gas mixture of between 60 and 80 per cent oxygen to ensure the meat keeps its bright red colour. This does not mean that the deterioration is being disguised but that the process of decay is delayed. The carbon dioxide also present in the gas mix inhibits bacterial growth.

MAP gas

Carbon dioxide inhibits the growth of most aerobic (respire with oxygen) bacteria and moulds. However, CO_2 is absorbed by fats and water, so if the level is too high the flavour of the food may become impaired or moisture will be lost causing the packaging to collapse. A minimum of 20 per cent CO_2 is recommended. Nitrogen is used to exclude air, particularly oxygen, and to help prevent the collapse of the

Modified atmosphere packaging is now used to package a wide range of products.

packaging. Controlled quantities of oxygen are required to maintain a natural colour, to allow the respiration of natural products (such as fruit and vegetables) and to prevent the growth of anaerobic (respire without oxygen) organisms.

MAP materials

A range of different materials is used for the packaging of MAP products and are often used together in layers. These include polyester (PET), nylon, polyvinylidene chloride (PVdC) and ethylene vinyl alcohol copolymer (EVOH). The materials must prevent the gases being lost and act as a barrier to water vapour to prevent the food from drying out. The packaging must also withstand the heat often used in **hermetic sealing** and it may need to be transparent so that the consumer can see what is inside. An anti-mist coating is sometimes applied to transparent materials to prevent water droplets forming on the inside of the packet.

MAP foods

Modified atmosphere packaging involves the use of a variety of materials, different combinations of gases and a range of methods in applying the packaging. This diversity means that MAP techniques can be applied to many different types of foods, such as:

- raw meat, offal, poultry, game (e.g. pheasant), fish and seafood
- cooked and cured meat (e.g. bacon), poultry, game, fish and seafood
- **cookchill** and readymeals
- fresh pasta
- cheeses (soft, hard and ready-grated)
- bakery products
- dried foods
- cooked vegetables, fresh fruit and vegetables
- liquid food (e.g. soup), beverages, carbonated soft drinks.

Products packaged using MAP techniques tend to be more expensive and, of course, the additional packaging means they are not very friendly towards the environment.

food labels

Label law

It may seem obvious that manufacturers label food products because consumers need to know what they are buying. However, exactly what is put on a food label and how it is worded is carefully controlled in the UK by the Food Labelling Regulations, 1996. These regulations apply to all food for human consumption (except natural mineral waters which have their own regulations). However, detailed labelling does not apply to certain foods, including honey, hens' eggs, cocoa and chocolate products and some sugar products.

Information that needs to appear on food products must be:
- on the packaging, or
- on a label attached to the pack, or
- on a label that is clearly visible through the packaging.

All food products requiring detailed labelling must be marked as shown below.

Datemarks

Use-by dates are shown on highly perishable foods that could be a safety risk if kept or eaten beyond this date. Foods labelled with these dates include fresh meat, fish and cheese. Best-before dates are usually found on foods that can be kept longer than a few days and, if kept or eaten beyond this date, may not be dangerous to health, although they will not be at their best. Foods labelled with these dates include breakfast cereals, biscuits and canned foods.

Give it a name

In many 'design and make it' activities at school, students are asked to come up with a suitable name for their new food product. In fact, even the naming of food

▼ *Labelling on food products is strictly regulated in the UK.*

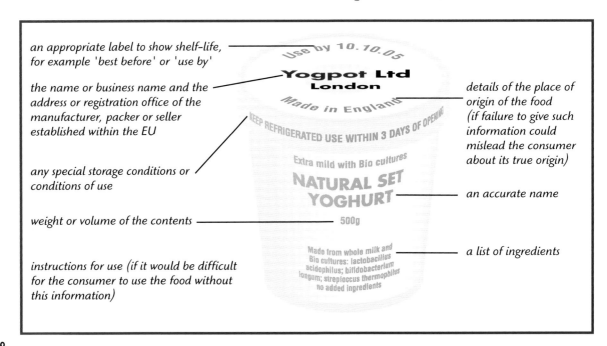

an appropriate label to show shelf-life, for example 'best before' or 'use by'

the name or business name and the address or registration office of the manufacturer, packer or seller established within the EU

any special storage conditions or conditions of use

weight or volume of the contents

instructions for use (if it would be difficult for the consumer to use the food without this information)

Use by 10.10.05

Yogpot Ltd
London

Made in England

KEEP REFRIGERATED USE WITHIN 3 DAYS OF OPENING

Extra mild with Bio cultures

NATURAL SET YOGHURT

500g

Made from whole milk and Bio cultures: lactobacillus acidophilus; bifidobacterium longum; streptococcus thermophilus no added ingredients

details of the place of origin of the food (if failure to give such information could mislead the consumer about its true origin)

an accurate name

a list of ingredients

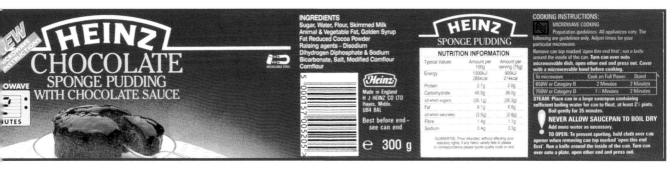

NUTRITION INFORMATION		
Typical Values	Amount per 100g	Amount per serving (75g)
Energy	1200kJ/ 285kcal	900kJ/ 214kcal
Protein	2.7g	2.0g
Carbohydrate	48.0g	36.0g
(of which sugars)	(35.1g)	(26.3g)
Fat	9.1g	6.8g
(of which saturates)	(3.5g)	(2.6g)
Fibre	1.4g	1.1g
Sodium	0.4g	0.3g

▲ *Food labels provide information about the product
and can include cooking instructions.*

is subject to labelling regulations. Food names are divided into three categories:

1 Names prescribed by law. For example, the species of a fish must be stated, e.g. plaice
2 Names that are customary. This is a name that is accepted by consumers, for example Yorkshire Pudding
3 Names that are not prescribed by law and are not customary names. These names must be chosen so that the consumer gets a sense of the product's 'true nature', meaning an accurate description of the food's main characteristics. In the case of a product name like Mars® bar, the name is followed by 'milk chocolate with soft nougat and caramel centre'.

Do not mislead

Under the Food Labelling Regulations 1996, manufacturers are restricted when making claims about their food products. Claims must not be made in the labelling or advertising of a food unless they fit the guidelines. Even a claim that is implied (rather than being explicit) is not acceptable. Claims might relate to nutrients such as protein, vitamins, minerals, **cholesterol**, energy or the slimming properties of a food.

Many 'slimmer's products' have a statement saying they can only help to reduce weight when eaten as part of a **calorie**-controlled diet.

Labelling nutrients

Nutritional labelling refers to any information appearing on a label that relates to any of the following: energy value, protein, carbohydrate, fat, fibre, sodium, vitamins or minerals. However, manufacturers are only allowed to include values for vitamins and minerals if the content is a 'significant amount' (15 per cent of the recommended daily allowance supplied by 100g or 100ml, or per package for single portions).

A nutrition claim is any statement, suggestion or implication in the labelling (or advertising) of a food that mentions the nutritional properties in relation to the energy and/or nutrients it does or does not provide, or that says it provides them in a higher or lower quantity than usual. Nutritional labelling is optional, unless a nutrition claim is being made.

Kellogg's packaging

A healthy start

The food company Kellogg's started life at the end of the 19th century when an American physician called Dr John Harvey Kellogg wanted to develop an easy-to-digest breakfast for his patients. This idea was so successful that by 1924 Kellogg's Cornflakes™ and All-Bran were being supplied to UK consumers from the USA. Clearly, Kellogg's have had many years' experience in the development, production, packaging and marketing of food products.

Pulling power

According to Kellogg's, when it comes to packaging the packet is probably the most important tool in the 'marketing mix' (that is, all aspects involved in marketing a product from advertising to free samples). It is the manufacturer's opportunity to influence consumers and, hopefully, to persuade them to buy their own brand rather than a competitor's. It has been shown in surveys in America that 70 per cent of sales in supermarkets are impulse purchases, so the pulling power of the packet is very real!

Costing and testing

One important consideration when researching a packaging design is the budget. The launch of a new product is likely to afford a higher budget than if an existing design is just to undergo small changes. A new packet can be tested in many ways, for example to test the shape, design appeal and product name. The retailer or consumer may be asked for their opinion of the product.

Define your market

All products need to be produced and advertised to a **consumer target group**. For example, Kellogg's Ricicles are aimed at the up-to-seven-year age group (the majority of Rice Krispies eaters are under twelve years whereas cornflakes are regarded as a family product with no specific age category). The first step in packaging design is to define the market, for example is it for adults, teenagers or all the family? Is it a specialized product for a particular section of consumers? This information is usually obtained by carrying out thorough consumer research.

Choose your material

The next consideration is the material from which the packaging is to be made. There is a range of materials to choose from (see pages 32–35) and the decision will be influenced by many factors.

◀ *The way food products are packaged can influence a consumer's decision about their purchase.*

◀ *Kellogg's have expanded their range of breakfast products in order to meet the needs of different consumer groups.*

Kellogg's suggest these factors might include:
1 the shelf-life required
2 the retail selling price (price at which the item is sold to the consumer)
3 the defined market
4 product protection
5 trade custom (competitive products)

Trade custom is a new consideration that has come about due to technological advances and the increase in the competitive retail world. Many products can be associated with a traditional type of packaging, for example bread was always wrapped in wax paper but now can be found in cellophane or polyethene. Kellogg's believe that in a highly competitive situation it may be desirable to fly in the face of trade custom and choose a novel type of packaging that gives you the edge over competitors. However, it is essential that the new packaging is superior to the established type.

Product quantity

The minimum quantity that can be packed is the smallest amount needed by the consumer. The maximum quantity is limited by the cost and product's shelf-life. Two sizes could be produced in order to satisfy a wide range of consumers.

Packaging shape

The shape of a packet may be influenced by the type of packaging machinery available or the shape of the product itself. However, during the development of many products, especially those aimed at children, there is the freedom to experiment with new, eye-catching packs. Kellogg's recommends that the following factors should be considered when thinking about shape.
1 Does the pack include a broad face on the shelves to get maximum exposure?
2 Will it stack well to get the most stock possible on display?
3 If points 1 and 2 are satisfied, will it suit the consumer when it is put to use?
4 Does it have an after-use?
5 Does it have novelty?

AIDA

Package design should fulfil the following criteria:

A – attract Attention
I – create Interest
D – stimulate Desire
A – translate desire into Action

When designing packaging, Kellogg's advise having the complete range of products available, including the competitors; to use colour illustration and lettering to attract consumers but avoid too many gimmicks or too much detail, and to try out the new design in a store fixture to see how well it works.

new developments

Population explosion

The population of the UK increased by half between 1901 and 1996. In 1998–99 the total population for the UK was 57.5 million. This is a staggering number of people, all of whom are demanding food on a daily basis. If food and drink were wanted purely to satisfy hunger and thirst, the task perhaps would not be so onerous. But people are insisting on products that meet a whole range of demands, including low cost, high quality, variety, **aesthetically** pleasing and easy preparation and cooking. The over-population of the UK is behind the current drive to use technology that can satisfy the culinary demands of the nation.

▼ *Today's massive population means the demand for food is greater than ever.*

Food processing

The food industry uses technology in a variety of ways. Sometimes it is just used to speed up a basic process such as rapidly washing and peeling vegetables that would otherwise have to be prepared by hand. But new techniques have also been developed in order to offer consumers alternative ways to eat, for example by producing chips that can be cooked in the oven. Such food processing includes any action that changes or converts raw plant or animal products into safe, edible and palatable items of food. It also enables the shelf-life of many foods to be extended. In reality, it is unlikely that the needs of today's massive population could be met without the use of food-processing techniques and, without it, we would certainly enjoy far less variety in our diet.

Food processing is not about **splicing genes** and bombarding foods with **additives**. Most of the foods we buy today have undergone some form of processing, such as the pasteurization of milk or the drying of grapes to form sultanas. For many consumers, the worry over food processing is not due to its existence but more to do with their lack of knowledge about exactly what is going on in the food industry. The BSE (bovine spongiform encephalalopathy) crisis and other recent food scares have influenced consumers' attitudes towards food products and have seriously affected the food industry, as well as the farming industry, as sales of certain products have fallen.

Food Standards Agency

In April 2000 the UK government set up a Food Standards Agency and gave it the task of raising the standards of food in the UK. It is an independent agency and is run by people with expertise in food safety. It works for consumers in order to:

> 'protect public health from risks which may arise in connection with the consumption of food, and otherwise to protect the interests of consumers in relation to food'.

The Agency has to report its findings to the government's health ministers but it can also publish any advice it gives to the government. Consumers can contact the Agency if they have any specific concerns over a food matter.

Consumer power

Consumer groups have become increasingly concerned about the way foods high in fat, sugar and salt are

The Food Standards Agency was set up to:

- provide advice and information to the public and to the government on food safety from farm to fork, nutrition and diet
- protect consumers through effective enforcement and monitoring
- support consumer choice through promoting accurate and meaningful labelling.

constantly being advertised during children's television. So much so, that the Food Standards Agency has now published a report stating the serious implications for the long-term health of children. This includes them being at greater risk of heart disease, cancer and diabetes in adult life. The Agency now recommends a code of practice to be drawn up with the food industry, focusing on most of the foods aimed at children, such as sweets, snack foods and soft drinks.

Research by the Food Standards Agency has also highlighted consumer concern over food labelling. A recent survey showed that 79 per cent of people surveyed thought meat was the most important food to be labelled with the country of origin and 91 per cent agreed that people have a right to know the country of origin of food.

Genetically modified (GM) ingredients also proved to be an area of interest for many consumers. As a result, the Food Standards Agency want changes to European food labelling and tighter control on claims about GM ingredients. The Agency also hopes to clear up the confusion for consumers over health claims such as 'low-fat', and 'fat-free'.

resources

Contacts

The Vegetarian Society
Parkdale
Dunham Road
Altrincham
Cheshire WA14 4QG
0161 928 0793
fax: 0161 926 9182
www.vegsoc.org.
A source of 'reference, motivation and encouragement' for anyone interested in issues of vegetarianism. Provides information, leaflets, recipes etc.

The Coeliac Society
PO Box 220
High Wycombe
Bucks
HP11 2HY
01494 437278
www.coeliac.co.uk
Provides information about coeliac disease.

Foodsense
London
SE99 7TT
Produce a wide range of free leaflets related to food matters. Titles include About Food Additives, Food Allergy and other Unpleasant Reactions to Food, Healthy Eating and Understanding Food Labels.

Diabetes UK
10 Queen Anne Street
London
W1G 9LH
020 7323 1531
www.diabetes.org.uk
Offers information and leaflets about diabetes.

British Sandwich Association
8 Home Farm
Ardington
Oxfordshire
OX12 8PN
www.sandwich.org.uk
The BSA is the 'voice' of the sandwich industry. It is mainly involved in safeguarding the integrity of the industry but also provides information and promotes the increased consumption of sandwiches.

Eating Disorders Association
First Floor
Wensum House
103 Prince of Wales Road
Norwich
Norfolk NR1 1DW
Helpline: 01603 621414 (9am – 6.30pm Mon-Fri)
Youth helpline: 01603 765050
(4pm – 6pm Mon-Fri)
www.edauk.com
The EDA provides telephone helplines, information sheets, leaflets and newsletters and runs a national network of self-help groups. They are able to advise on both bulimia and anorexia.

I.C.T

www.doh.gov.uk/ohn/ohnhome.htm
The Government's website giving details of the white paper Saving Lives: Our Healthier Nation and current health targets.

www.foodstandards.gov.uk
The Government's information website for the Food Standards Agency containing details of their aims, research, committees, regulations, press releases etc. as well as details about how to contact them.

www.ontheline.org.uk
A millennium project which focuses attention on the future of our planet and on our role as global citizens. It provides an opportunity for people in the UK to get to know more about the eight diverse countries that lie on the Greenwich Meridian Line – the UK, France, Spain, Algeria, Mali, Burkina Faso, Togo and Ghana. It includes a range of activities involving schools, local communities, artists and film-makers. It explores the life and culture in all eight countries.

Places to visit

Museum of Advertising & Packaging
The Albert Warehouse
Gloucester Docks
Gloucester GL1 2EH
01452 302309
Britain's first museum of advertising and packaging holds the Robert Opie Collection. About 300,000 items relating to the history of our consumer society are on display providing a fascinating insight into the British way of life over the past hundred years.

glossary

additives something that is not usually used as a food but is added during the production of a food, either to aid production or to enhance the product in some way (e.g. appearance, texture)

aesthetic relates to the beauty or artistic nature of something, such as a creatively arranged plate of food

ambient refers to a temperature. Ambient foods are found on supermarket shelves and include tinned products, UHT products and dried products.

amino acids proteins are made up of simpler substances called amino acids, some of which are essential in the growth and development of our bodies. Amino acid molecules are joined together to form long chains.

anaphylactic shock rare but life-threatening allergic reaction. It occurs in people with an extreme sensitivity to a particular substance (allergen). The sufferer must be given an injection of adrenaline as soon as possible.

calorie measurement of energy used in nutrition; one calorie of heat raises the temperature of 1ml of water through 1°C. Units of 1000 calories are written as calories or kilocalories (kcals). Nutritionists today often use kilojoule and megajoule (a joule is the amount of energy exerted when a force of 1 newton is moved through a distance of 1 metre) 1 calorie = 4.18 joules; KJ = 1000 joules. MJ = 1000 kjoules.

cholesterol fatty substance naturally present in the body

consumer target group group of consumers being targeted when marketing a product. The group could be a certain age range (for example, babies) or a type of consumer (for example, vegetarian).

cookchill food products that are rapidly chilled immediately after cooking, and then transported and stored at a chilled temperature until they are reheated by the consumer

coronary heart disease when the blood (and therefore oxygen) supply to a part of the heart is gradually impeded by a narrowing of the vessels supplying the heart caused by fatty substances, including cholesterol

disposable income money people may have available to them after they have paid for essential items

ester chemical name for compounds formed from an acid and an alcohol

fasting when food is not eaten, for example for religious reasons such as during Ramadam. The word 'breakfast' was originally used because eating breakfast represented 'breaking the fast' that occurred during the night.

fortified fortified foods and drinks have had nutrients added during processing. Fortified foods include breakfast cereals that have had vitamins and minerals added. These nutrients have to be included on the ingredients list.

genetic to do with genes which affect heredity

genetically modified ingredients which have had genes moved or transplanted from another plant or animal in order to improve a characteristic such as colour or texture

hermetic seal a closure in packaging that prevents food from being contaminated by the environment. It is created using heat and/or pressure.

importation systems methods used to buy in and transport foods from one country to another

leach out to move out of one substance and into another; for example, vitamins leach out of vegetables and into the cooking water when they are boiled in too much water for too long

modified atmosphere packaging (MAP) packaging technology in which the atmosphere inside a container is altered to extend the shelf-life of the product but retain all the food's natural characteristics (such as its colour)

monosaccharides simple sugars containing one saccharide unit. When joined together they form disaccharides and polysaccharides. All of these sugars are carbohydrates.

non-starch polysaccharide (NSP) complex carbohydrates found in foods other than starches; also called fibre or dietary fibre. NSPs may be divided into insoluble (found in wheat, maize, rice) and soluble (found in oats, beans, rye). Vegetables and fruit usually contain both types.

novel protein a protein food that has been developed from new sources; for example, vegetarian protein foods produced from micro-organisms, fungi and algae

patent form of registration showing that a person owns the sole right to a product or process

pathological causing disease

peer group people of a similar age

permeable describes an item that will allow substances such as a gas or a liquid to pass through it

psychological in the mind; for example, if a food was eaten just before a person was ill, the person may then associate the food with illness and have an adverse reaction when eating it; there is no physical cause, as in the case of a food allergy or intolerance

risk factor something which contributes to the risk of a disease or illness. For example, smoking, lack of exercise, high blood pressure and a high fat diet are all risk factors for coronary heart disease.

saturated fat saturated fats have a higher proportion of saturated fatty acids than unsaturated fatty acids. Their structure means that each carbon chain has its full complement of hydrogen atoms (it is saturated with them). These fats are mainly from animal sources and are solid at room temperature (butter, lard, fat on meat, or meat fat).

splicing genes altering genes during food production by making a copy of a desirable gene and putting it into another plant or animal

staple principal food, particularly of a country or region, usually high in carbohydrate; for example, rice is a staple food of China

textured vegetable protein (TVP) vegetable protein usually made to resemble meat

trimester a three-monthly period into which a full-term pregnancy is divided. The first three months are called the first trimester, months four to six are the second trimester and the final trimester consists of the seventh, eighth and ninth months.

index